Feelings

Written by Monica Hughes
Illustrated by Naomi Tipping

Collins

I like to sit and look at a book.

I like to go out with my dad.
I like to run and jump and kick.

I feel sad in the dark.

I like it if I can get my torch.

I was fond of my gran.

She got ill and died.
I cried and cried.

I stamp around if I get mad.

I run and yell and shout out loud.

I feel sad if my dad and
mum shout.

I like it if he hugs her and
we all go out.

I feel proud if I sing a song.

I blush if I get a big clap.

Feelings

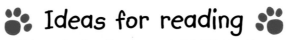

Ideas for reading

Written by Sue Graves cert. Ed (Distinction)
Primary Literacy Consultant

Reading objectives:
- use phonic knowledge to decode regular words and read them aloud accurately
- read and understand simple sentences
- demonstrate understanding when talking with others about what they have read

Communication and language objectives:
- listen to stories, accurately anticipating key events and respond to what they hear with relevant comments, questions or actions
- express themselves effectively, showing awareness of listeners' needs
- answer "how" and "why" questions about their experiences and in response to stories or events

Curriculum links: Personal, social and emotional development

Focus phonemes: ou (shout, out), ee (feeling), ie (died, cried), or (torch)

Other new phonemes: ar, er, ou, th (this), ng, w, oo (look), y

Fast words: I, like, to, a, go, my, the, of, we, all

Word count: 107

Build a context for reading

- Write the words that feature the focus phonemes *ou, ee, ie* and *or* on a small whiteboard and ask the children to fast-read them, blending aloud if they need to.

- Choose three fast words from the section above, e.g. *I, my, we.* Ask the children to fast-read these words.

- Look at the front cover. Ask them to read the title together. *What do they think this book is about?* Ask the children if they think this is a fiction or non-fiction book. Encourage them to give reasons.

Understand and apply reading strategies

- Give each child a copy of the book. Invite them to read it independently.

- Listen to each child read as you move around the group. Remind children to blend the phonemes in words they find difficult to read.

- Ask fast-finishers to make a list of all the things that make them feel happy. Point out that it may not be when they are given a present or a treat, but may be when they play with their friends, or see a grandparent they haven't seen for a while.

- As you move round the group, check that children can decipher new words, e.g *died* and *fond* and that they understand the meanings of them.